D0898901

BUTTON BUTTON

Who Has the Button?

by Ruth Harriet Jacobs, Ph.D.

crones' own press

NASHUA PUBLIC

812
J
copy 1
NPL

Copyright ©1983 by Ruth Harriet Jacobs. All rights reserved.
Second Printing, 1988.

MY GRANDMOTHER MARMITA, originally published in *New Directions for Women,* Sept/Oct 1982

I, ONCE BRIEFLY A DAUGHTER, originally published in *Clark NOW,* Vol. 12 #3, 1982

FROM MY MOTHER, originally published in *Clark NOW,* Fall 1982

EVEN AS I WRITE THIS, originally published as "Neighbor" in *1982 Anthology of Massachusetts Poetry Association*

BEFORE WE ARE ACCUSTOMED, titled "Older Women" published in *Sojourner,* Dec. 1979

THE GENTLE BEARDED YOUNG MAN is an excerpt from poem "The Eighties" published in *Sociologists for Women in Society Magazine,* Vol. 12, #1, Jan. 1982

FUNCTIONARIES, originally in American Sociological Association's *Footnotes.* Oct. 1977

SEVENTY IS BEING OUTSIDE, first published in *New Directions for Women,* Sept/Oct 1982

I SHALL BE FREE AS YOU WOULD HAVE ME FREE, first published as "Patient's Promise" in *Women and Therapy,* Vol. 1, No. 2, Summer 1982

The poetic lines of Beth and Lois, pp. 64 through 67 are from the poet's long poem, "Twenty Years After" in *Peace is our Profession,* East River Anthology, 1981

Library of Congress Cataloging in Publication Data

Jacobs, Ruth
    Button, button, who has the button?
    I Title

88-47650

PS3560.A2557B8   1988   811'.54   85-22394

ISBN 0-9615216-3-5
paper edition
Printed in the United States of America

Crones' Own Press
310 Driver Street
Durham, N.C. 27703

Cover design by Galia Goodman
Text design by Elizabeth Freeman, Nancy Webster and Jennifer Potts

ABOUT PERFORMANCE AND ROYALTIES

This poetic drama is for reading to yourself or for reading aloud. It is moving when read aloud from scripts. It does not have to be memorized.

This play may be presented as a whole with an intermission beetween the two acts or parts may be used. Discussion may or may not follow the play, depending on your audience and circumstances. It is useful for classes, meetings, conferences as well as theater audiences. Various scenes may be presented alone as experiences and discussion starters. Many colleges and religious, women's and aging organizations have used the play.

Scenes which can stand alone are scenes two and three in act one and scene one in act two. Some groups have presented, with good success, the whole of act one and other groups have presented with good success a combination of scene one and scene two from act one or a combination of scene two and three from act one.

For older women themselves or service providers, some groups have used from page 23 where Mary asks "Who am I?" through to the end of scene three. This part of scene three also appears in Ruth Jacobs' manual for group leaders *Older Women Surviving and Thriving* available for $17.95 plus $2 mailing from Family Service America, 11700 W. Lake Park Drive, Milwaukee, Wisconsin 53224.

There are no royalties required for presenting this play if no admission is charged by a non-profit organization. However, if admission is charged, even by a non-profit, royalties should be arranged with the author, Ruth Jacobs, 75 High Ledge Avenue, Wellesley, Mass., 02181, Phone 617-237-1793. She is also available to lead discussions of the play or speak on women's issues.

Acknowledgements

All poems in the play are by the author. She would like to thank three artists' colonies for providing retreats so that she might work on the poetry and the play itself: The Edna St. Vincent Millay Colony, Ossabaw Island Foundation and Alfred University Summer Place. She would like also to thank the women of the National Summer Place. She would also like to thank the women of the National Chemical Distributors Association and the following individuals for suggestions and encouragement: Edith Jane Jacobs, daughter of the author, Ruth M. Murphy, M.D., Claire R. Cohen, Laura Lein, Peggy McIntosh, Carol Burdick, Pia Raffaele, Ellie Mamber, Julia and Gobin Stair, Elizabeth and David Dodson Grey and Rosalyn Feldberg. She would also like to thank Beacon Press, 25 Beacon Street, Boston, Massachusetts 02108 which published her prose book *Life After Youth: Female, Forty, What Next?* The play does not duplicate the book but the research for the book generated the play. She also wishes to thank the Wellesley College Center for Research on Women which premiered the mother/ daughter segment completed in February, 1983. She thanks Elizabeth Freeman for believing in the play and Galia Goodman for designing the cover.

Cast In Order Of Appearance

(Note: Whenever possible, the cast should be women of color as well as white women and women of all ethnic groups possible. However, the mother and daaughter (Lisa and Ellen) and the Thin Woman and Fat Woman should be paired for similar characteristics.

RUTH, representing the author, a woman about 60

MARMITA, an elderly woman

JANE, a woman about 50

THE CHORUS, made up of women of all types or one woman representing a chorus of women's voices

ELLEN, a woman about 40

LISA, a woman about 50

JENNIFER, a woman about 30, (she should *not* be blond)

MARY, a woman about 50

VIRGINIA, a woman about 60

ELIZABETH, a woman about 70

DORA, a woman about 80

THIN WOMAN, middle ageed

FAT WOMAN, middle aged

HELENE, a woman about 50

PSYCHIATRIST (Female)

CATHERINE, a woman about 50

SARA, a woman about 35

CONSUELO, a woman about 45 (Hispanic)

LOIS, a woman about 55

BETH, a woman about 25

SISTER MARY CARITA (Wears headcovering, cross, and short habit or simple dress.)

ACT ONE

INTERMISSION IF DESIRED

ACT TWO

ACT ONE

Scene I

Who Speaks for Women?

Wearing a simple outfit with a long tangled chain of buttons around her neck, Ruth walks onto the stage slowly, looks around at the audience and says:)

> I am full of the voices of women.
> For nearly sixty years
> I have traveled this country
> and my life
> many lives
> listening.
> I must tell the stories of women
> who cannot speak for themselves
> who have been silenced
> or have spoken
> and not been heard.

Their voices exult, cry, plead, laugh, sigh, sing, assent and assert. Though the women's voices have individual tones and tunes, their words and themes are indeed a chorus. My cantata is this chorus. But first you need to know about this woman before you who dares and cares to speak for women. We can only offer others what we are. Everything we see or say is filtered through our own lives

> I parted my hair on the left side
> the hair I had worn on the right
> but the roots in stubborn treason
> had directed it back by night.

I am Ruth Harriet, granddaughter of Harriet who died before I was born, and granddaughter of Marmita and daughter of Jane. We all go back to our foremothers, though we often deny this. Let me tell about Marmita, born in Kiev, the Ukraine. She came to Ellis Island where European immigrants to the United States were processed early in this century by officials who couldn't cope with foreign names.

My grandmother, Marmita
was given the name Minnie
at Ellis Island
and carefully traced it
on the report cards
of five children.
It was all the English
she could ever write.

When her oldest child,
my mother, died at thirty
she took a ten year old
and a three year old
and traced Minnie
on our report cards
and on all those forms
to get legal guardianship
and state aid to feed us.

She crocheted scarves
for the social workers
begged clothes and camps
and within a slum
kept a shining house.

Half-crazed
by her daughter's death
and endless poverty
she cried, screamed,
had no patience
with my brother
and even threatened me
too good though I was.

But every spring
somewhere in that slum

> she stole lilacs
> to put upon my bureau
> and trace her love
> forever on me.

It is only recently that I wrote that poem. I have just begun to understand my grandmother as I have myself aged. I empathize as I see what it is to be a woman whose options are limited by age, gender, roles and fate.

One morning last year I searched in my Grandmother's button jar to match a button. Grandma gave me the jar shortly before her death at age 87, decades ago. As I sifted through the buttons, I realized how old some were. I also had visions of her life. There were buttons cut from the clothes she sewed from necessity for her five children and from friends' hand-me-downs she altered for my brother and me. I remembered she had sewed late at night, exhausted after her day's chores. Yet women like her had been unvalued and not counted as part of the labor force because they had worked at home.

In the jar were military buttons cut from the uniforms of her sons with tears and relief after the wars. There were several glittering buttons saved from the few good dresses she had owned, bought for her children's high school graduations and weddings.

Suddenly, I, certainly no craftsperson, needed desperately to make something from my grandmother's buttons. Though my college students' papers waited, I began in a compulsive, even frenzied way to string the buttons on strong thread. Without forethought, I strung the buttons in a random way and then tangled them together as Grandma's life was strung and tangled not by her design or desire but by the needs of others.

(Marmita enters.)

MARMITA: Yes, I really never had much choice. In Russia, I loved a young man, but my parents instead made me marry your Grandfather. I never really loved Avrom. But I did my duty. When he was jailed for opposing the Czar, I bribed the guard and went to the jail wearing two sets of clothes and smuggled my husband out in women's clothes.

Then I left everybody I cared about in Russia to escape by steerage with him to America. After all, he was the father of my child, your mother.

I was only twenty but had already had three infants and your mother was the only one who lived. My first daughter died shortly after birth as did your mother's boy twin. It was my second pregnancy in two years. I was worn out and did not have enough milk to feed both twins. In those days there was only breast feeding. Your mother was the frailer twin so I gave the boy to a strong peasant woman to nurse. It was a hard choice. She fed her own baby first and there was not enough for my boy.

You know all my life I saved everything but I couldn't save my own children. Five of my seven children, those two babies, and your mother and another daughter and a son died before me. And it was so hard to bring them up. Your grandfather never made a good living. I shopped so frugally. I sewed and took in boarders. During prohibition I made and sold wine. But it wasn't that dangerous. The police were my best customers and they protected me.

When my son enlisted in the Marines below the legal age, and was sent to fight in Nicaragua, I went to the Mayor and got him out. But I couldn't save your mother when she got cancer and died. I used to go to the park and cry so she would not see me. When we were together, I pretended I didn't know she was dying and she pretended she didn't know. She must have cried alone too.

RUTH: It would have been better for you both if you had not hidden it and had cried together.

MARMITA: Maybe, but in those days it was different and we kept our feelings secret. But it got harder and harder not to cry openly when your Uncle George and your Aunt Ida died. It made me crazy angry and I blamed their mates, everybody, the world. When your father collapsed, it was hard to take care of you and your brother but I think being needed kept me going.

I always wanted to be needed. When I was old and even poorer, I used to walk around the city streets looking for handkerchiefs men had dropped. I would wash and iron the handkerchiefs and give them to you for your husband so I would have something to give you.

RUTH: You gave me courage. You taught me how to go on when my firstborn died as a toddler. And when you insisted on being in the old age home because you didn't want to burden anyone, you begged me to bring you my family's clothes to mend and I did even if I had to pull off buttons or rip the clothes first. You made me so many afghans that I had no places to put them. And you worried when I got three university degrees between 35 and 45 that I was neglecting my children. You didn't see a need for higher education for women, especially married ones. How were you to know that my marriage and support would end in divorce after thirty years?

(Marmita leaves. Jane comes on stage.)

JANE: When I was dying those two years and you and your brother were so small, I was insane with pain and worry about what would happen to you two. When you didn't take care of your brother or clean the house, I said to you "You will be sorry when I am dead." And then I felt guilty. Did I make you feel guilty?

RUTH: Yes. It took me years and much help to get over that. I am still not over it completely. But you couldn't help it. You also loved me and I you and I named my daughter after you.

> I, once briefly a daughter,
> now always a daughter
> dream of daughter.
> She is the mirror
> in which I see
> my mother's eyes
> look back at me.

I was only ten when you died but you had given me enough by then to make a life on. And other women gave me what you could not.

> From my mother
> the love of poems
> and violets.
> From my grandmother
> giving when
> there was little
> left to give.
> From one aunt
> an artist's eye
> and from another,
> courage despite
> recurrent tragedy.
> From a near-mother,
> competence at work
> and from still
> another nurturer

7

keeping compassion
within the bounds
of self-respect.

JANE: Did my friends help you?

RUTH: Oh, I forgot that. Yes, the dentist's wife made her husband fill Larry's teeth and mine free. Another made her husband give me my first job. A third bought me a winter coat.

The motherless
have many
mothers.

It wasn't surprising. Through life, women often help others. I experienced this after my divorce when I moved into an Italian-American neighborhood full of nurturers.

Across the yards
abundant with tomatoes
zucchini, eggplant, peppers
and the blessed grape,
my neighbors' Italian voices
comfort me with liquid sounds.

Domenic, Adelina,
Joseph, Yolanda
call me Ruthie
wondering at this Jew,
this strange professor,
who types into the night.

Even as I write this,
the phone rings.
It is Adelina, eighty-two
who senses I think of her
and tells me not to cook.
She is bringing pasta
for my dinner
her perfect poem.

> She made me, a stranger,
> welcome here.
> Like her garden,
> I flourish with her love.

(Jane leaves.)

RUTH: As a child, I envied girls whose mothers took care of them. It was a mystery to me why so many hated their mothers. When I grew up, I wondered why adult women often disliked and avoided older women. Now, I understand. Women's lives in this society are often painful and young women see in their mothers their own future dilemmas.

Scene II

In Between: In the Middle

(The chorus recites. One woman can represent the chorus.)

I am a woman
in between
in the middle
pulled by others' tides
and even by my own.

In between waking and sleeping
in between sleeping and waking
halfway from birth to death
childhood and old age
I glimpse my strengths
and weaknesses
courage and fears
desires and limitations
joys and sorrows
hope and despair
fear and faith.

I am between
wanting marriage
and wanting singleness
wanting children
and wanting my time.

I am in the middle of
lovers and former lovers
siblings
parents and my children
my husband and my children
and his children
his parents and mine
the empty nest and the refilled
children and their spouses
children and their children
job and home
work and pleasure
work and more work
supervisor and supervisees
my husband's retirement and
my renaissance
friends and foes
friends and other friends
adulthood and studenthood
the generations before
and those ahead
home and the world.

I am torn between
ambition for my daughter
and knowledge of
the risks and costs
the rewards and
cruelties awaiting
as women assert
and are punished.

I am between
anxiety and confidence
activity and passivity
assertion and diffidence
trust and mistrust
hope and hopelessness
dreams and nightmares
love and hate
menstruation and menopause
triumph and defeat

growth and stagnation
nuturing and resenting
hurting and healing
self interest and selflessness
sensuality and celibacy
spirituality and intellectuality
dependence and independence
my thin and fat selves
relaxation and stress
humor and pathos
myself and others
and parts of myself.

I am in the middle of
war and peace
radicalism and conservatism
private concerns and political action
activism and retreatism
feminism and backlash
convenience and the environment
my country and universality.

I am a woman
in between
in the middle
pulled by others' tides
and even by my own.

I am a woman
in the middle
in between
wanting to help
and wanting help
happy
discontented
free
fettered
fearless
frightened
frank.

I am a woman

in between
who I was
and who
I shall yet be
I am Me
groaning
groping
growing
skimming the waters
testing the waters
swimming against the tides
sinking
surfacing
making splashes
getting wet
and wetting others.

I am in the middle
of a new ocean
but will not drown;
my ambivalences
will be islands
to rest upon
with other women
between our thrusts
toward a shore
as yet uncharted
and even denied.

I am a woman
in between
in the middle
pulled by others' tides
and even by my own.

(Enter Ellen, a mother and Lisa, her daughter.)

ELLEN: The poem applies to me.
                It is hard to be a mother

                        Who will feed the feeder
                        Who will nurture the nurturers

Who will help the helpers
Who will counsel the counselors
and when?

LISA: The poem applies to me.

It is hard to be a daughter
My mother is a mirror
of what I do not wish to be
I want no ambivalences

What of darkness fear I
if I know no fear?
What of weakness hear I
if I will not hear?
What of pain or sorrow
if I close my eyes
need I fear tomorrow?

ELLEN: Dream on little wise one
deny any weakling senses
waking life, my darling
silences defenses

LISA: What a pain you are.

You remind me of those homeless pitiful bag ladies wandering
around the streets carrying their rags in bags.

ELLEN: We are all bag ladies
or becoming so.
Nothing lasts
not love
or the beloved
or hope
even mountains crumble
only the ocean waits
to catch our tears

Bags of memories
tell us who we were
before we were wise

> The bags burden us.
> Carrying about
> our losses,
> we stumble
> clutching our unfreedom
> against all threats
> or promises
> it being all we have
> it being all we know
> it being all we are.

LISA: You sure feel sorry for yourself. You make me feel guilty for growing up. You make me want to get away from you even more.

> You should try harder
> You sound like a martyr.
> I suggest that you
> turn anger into art
> a crust of bread
> into bread pudding
> old chickens are tough
> they survived the axe
> even bag ladies manage
> why not you?

ELLEN: I do not like what I am.

> I have tried to find new roles.
> Men my age prefer you.
> Employers prefer you too.
> They seem to say:
>
> You can't trust older women
> they put philodendron
> on the file cabinets
> dump real coffee grinds
> into wastebaskets
> and even hang posters
> in the washrooms.
>
> Next thing you know
> they will be asking

for a raise because
they made the place
feel like someplace
you might like to be
if they weren't there
looking down noses
when you cheat or lie
to the customers.

LISA: I think you exaggerate this age discrimination bit. Older women aren't
the only ones who have problems. Young women have troubles too.

ELLEN: I know.

Before we are accustomed
to our bodies and our minds
they are after them.
We nurture before we are
comfortable in our skins.

Then, when we know
the joys of flesh
and wisdom shared
we are eager to meet
a world that has
lost interest.

LISA: I sure know what you mean. Guys are after us all the time. Being young
and pretty isn't always a bargain. You have to fend them off. It must be
hard though when they aren't there to fend off.

I worry sometimes.
Will this long hair
turn grey and dry?
Will my Prince Charming
turn into a frog?
Should I even worry about such trivia?
I went to Seabrook
and to New York to demonstrate
but they didn't really hear.
Will there be a world left
for me to grow old in?

Should I have children
will they be able to grow up?

ELLEN: Are you really that discouraged?

LISA: It is not like the seventies, Mom.

The gentle bearded young men
have gone into the corporate offices
or are driving taxis
toward the graveyard
of their dreams for social change.

The long haired women in ragged jeans
have cut their hair and hopes
and joined the secretarial
or data processing pool.

The libraries are being boarded up
the teachers sent from the schools
public transport is in trouble
public welfare is dead
and social justice also.

ONLY MUNITIONS PROSPER

ELLEN: And I thought you and your friends had it all. I think it was simpler for
my mother, your grandmother. God knows she worked hard doing for
others and suffered sexism but she thought things would be better for
me and for you...Her generation believed in progress. Mine is discour-
aged. Yours believes in doom.

LISA: Oh, it's not that bad. Sometimes I worry about the world but mostly I
am concerned with me. I guess I really think the world will go on. In fact,
the major problem I feel is fear of failure, not measuring up and in some
way failing my standards. I feel pressure to do something special,
something definite and concrete with my life. Grandma didn't think she
had to do it all and have it all and maybe you didn't either and maybe
that was easier.

17

ELLEN: Well, I used to think that I shouldn't expect too much out of life but being a good wife and mother and friend and be good to others generally. Listen to how that feels now.

> Sometimes when
> exhausted by hard work
> and work for others
> I refuse to rest
> reminding myself
> that people
> in concentration camps
> dropped in exhaustion
> that refugees or POW's
> walked or rowed
> to death.
>
> I identify
> with the wretched
> making myself wretched
> punishing myself
> for imagined guilts
> driving myself
> serving others
> worrying about them
>
> Perhaps I am
> an exaggeration case
> but we share
> this woman syndrome.
> We were taught it
> and not just
> by our mothers.
>
> I deserve better
> daughter, you deserve better.
> I deserve, you deserve
> to rest when tired
> to eat when hungry
> good carefully chosen food
> nourishing instead of cheap
> or leftover.

I deserve, you deserve
self love
and being loved
I deserve my choices
and first choice.
I deserve a decent
humane society.
I deserve success
and rewards
I deserve to trust myself
as others trust me.
I deserve to forgive myself
as I forgive others.

I deserve
not to be stepped upon
and to cry out
when I hurt.
I deserve to have righteous
indignation
and to stop making excuses
for others
and start making them
for myself.

I deserve,
to allow myself
the seemingly trivial
I deserve new clothes
not always clothes on sale
I deserve fresh sheets
and fragrant flowers.

I deserve
you deserve
not to have to do
ABSOLUTELY EVERYTHING
AND FOR EVERYONE.

Although I will continue
concern for the wretched
I have a right to happiness.

I must take care of myself
as I continue to give
to others including you, daughter.

If I can only nurture others
if I cannot nurture myself
if I am tired all the time
what do I teach my daughter
what do we teach all our daughters
and our sons?

How much social change
is needed.
How much unlearning
we must do
to claim the joy
that is our right
our need
our survival!

LISA: I understand. I am glad you feel we deserve. I am sorry I am so hard on you. You've seen I am really scared though I've been afraid to show it. And I need to push you away so I can be free.

If only I could look at us
here, now and today, standing
as independent travelers
who shared a trip
now pasted neatly in an album
of casual reminiscence.

If only I no longer waited
to reenact that journey
exposed and small
as I was once
bringing you my infant hurts
and blaming you for them.

If only we could snap the cord
that pulls a raw red furrow
deep across your open heart and mine.
If only we could break that hateful rope

and yet not make of it a noose
to hang that tenderness
which once was what I grew upon,
that you and I might compromise
end this present bitter journey
embark upon some new and separate ones
keeping our luggage light and apart
greeting each other as we pass
and welcoming our new companions freely.

ELLEN: I know you must take your own journey to a place where I cannot go or choose even though I try to give you maps you refuse. Find that place and enjoy the finding. Sometimes I mourn my child gone and try to keep you as one. Please grow and go with as little pain as possible for both of us and with my love and pride.

LISA: Though now we stand against the door
reliving history once more,
I shall be free as you would have me free
and armed enough to bear the pain of parting
and leaving you, go on with hope to see
this present tense of life now starting.

Please know your gifts of life and love
are maps I take along
but I must feel by day and night
that I am I for once
and I am strong.

Mom, what will you do now?

ELLEN: I am not sure.

I am a woman
in between
in the middle
pulled by others' tides
and even by my own.

I am in the middle
of a new ocean
but will not drown

my ambivalences
will be islands
to rest upon
with other women
including you, daughter
between our thrusts
toward a shore
as yet uncharted
and even denied
BUT THERE IS A SHORE.

LISA:

I am a woman
in between
who I was
and who
I shall yet be
I am me
groaning
groping
growing
skimming the waters
testing the waters
swimming against the tides
sinking
sufacing
making splashes
getting wet
and wetting others
including you, mother   *(she laughs)*
AND I WILL NOT DROWN.

ELLEN and LISA
in unison

WE are women
in between
in the middle
of a troubled world
pulled by others' tides
and even by our own.

(Ellen and Lisa embrace. They remain on the stage.)

Scene Three:

Women Resting on Their Ambivalences

(Lisa and Ellen remain on the stage and are joined by five other women. One is about thirty, one about fifty, one about sixty, one about seventy and one about eighty. The women carry large, round brightly colored pillows and two of them carry extra pillows which they hand to Ellen and Lisa. The seven women seat themselves on the cushions in a semi-circle in the following order: Lisa, then Jennifer, the thirty year old, Ellen, then Mary, the fifty year old, then Virginia, the sixty year old, then Elizabeth, the seventy year old, and then Dora, the eighty year old.)

LISA: Sitting here feels like school. Remember when we sat and played button, button, who has the button? Well you just heard my story. Jennifer, you are the next oldest. You take the button.

(Lisa hands a large button to Jennifer.)

JENNIFER: So it is my turn.

                         Who am I?
                         I am what I do.
                         THEY pay me to be
                         SOMEBODY and that is
                         why my WORK is really me
                         and if you don't believe that
                         you haven't been brought up right.
                         You must be a foreignor or one of those
                         people left over from the early seventies
                         who thought we were going to find ourselves
                         someplace besides the office or on the couches.

LISA: Is that how you function?

JENNIFER: Functionaries
can only function
at functions.

Empty rooms
empty them
of roles.

Terrified,
they function
to create functions.

Functions thus
are functional
when empty.

Functionaries
are empty
though functioning.

Functionaries
deserve pity
for terror.

Who today
is not
a functionary?

Functioning
is after all
functional.

ELLEN: It sounds pretty grim.

JENNIFER: I get by.

Put work beside your bed
make lists
contract your services
do the extras

fill every hour
tell people
you are always busy
and be that way.

If you fall
asleep in the sun
drink coffee
and run.

LISA: I guess it has worked for you. You are a success.

JENNIFER: Yes, I suppose so, but:

The world's over ripe plums
splatter into weary hands
which hurl them on the ground
like bloody, useless things.
These are not the fruits desired
It is not enough to be admired.

Forget I said that. This is an off day for me and this group is where I let down. I really am lucky to have a decent job these days. I tell myself, "So what if there is no Mr. Right."

You had better settle for work
love is for the young
the blond
the lithe
the lucky
the others.

You are a workhorse
pulling weights
piling weights
putting weights
upon yourself.

Learn to love your work
or talk a good line.
Maybe someone will
pat you

                                    pet you
                                    "nice horsy."

ELLEN: You're not missing that much if you don't marry. I read somewhere that single women are the happiest, healthiest women in America. Marriage is better for men than women.

JENNIFER: Yes, Ellen, but the grass is always greener elsewhere.....You already talked so if you don't mind I'll give the button to Mary.

ELLEN: Okay.

(Jennifer gets up, passes the button to Mary and returns to her pillow.)

MARY: Who am I?

I was a wife for thirty years. One day my husband decided he didn't want to be married anymore to an older woman, though he was, of course, four years older than I. I've always thought it had something to do with the fact that his company passed him over for a promotion. He was stuck in a dead end job he hated while younger fellows were zooming past him. Anyway, he had affairs with women much younger than himself. Thank God our children were grown and out of the house. Finally, he made one woman half his age pregnant and he married her after our divorce. Now they have two babies and I suppose he feels important at home, if not at work.

As for me, I remember going shopping shortly after he left. I kept walking around the market without putting anything in my cart. Suddenly, I realized I didn't even know what I liked to eat. For years, I had been buying what he liked and what the children liked and that is what I ate. I didn't even know my own tastes in food. How was I going to make a life for myself? Though I was pretty depressed that Sunday I went to a singles' brunch I saw advertised in the newspaper. I got all dressed up. I guess I hoped to find a man.

Well, the woman who ran the club came up to me and said, "please don't come back, you're too old for this group." I looked around. The men were my age or lots older. I was devastated. Of course, I had grey hair then. *(She laughs)* I have colored it since.

LISA: What did you do besides color your hair?

MARY?   I cried a lot. At first it was utter despair.

> Leaving the suburb and wifehood
> for a cheaper city apartment,
> I moved my plants in first
> so something would greet me.
>
> The first morning I awoke
> at dawn to see the rats' ballet
> a strange and frenzied circle
> beneath my window and said
> "there are worse things than rats."

Strange things were happening to me.

> In what is one to believe?
> The city screams at you
> and you scream back,
> finding your voice
> someone else's shrill cry.

JENNIFER: I guess you were scared.

MARY: Yes and more than that.

> I envied those women
> whose husbands tucked them
> into cars and beds
> and paid their dinner checks.
> My so-called freedom
> felt like unconnectedness.
> I thought, some day
> I will stay in bed forever
> and no one will care
> or even know.

I hate married women and was foolish enough to think they were all happy. Once, I even wrote an imaginary letter to a suburbanite.

> You,
> with your small mouth
> and long tennis legs,

27

> living with antiques
> a husband and roses,
> don't know what it is
> to live alone on women's
> tiny wages that buy
> starches and roaches.
> Uncordially
> yours.

LISA: You had a right to be angry, I think.

MARY: Yes, and I wanted revenge.

Before I saw my former husband again:

> I wanted to be loved
> or at least desired
> and possessed
> so that the creeping mildew
> of soul and body
> would not be intensified
> by the sight and smell of him
> my lost and only lover
> of a long and wasted life
> destroyed by his rejection.

I covered up my pain with bravado. I thought:

> Not wanting to turn to salt,
> I won't look back.
> Salt is tears
> tears are acid rain
> and acid rain corrodes.

I told myself:

> There are other fish in the sea
> and I will fry them.
> There are other rocks on the shore
> and I will throw them.
> There are other men in the world
> and I will try them.

But it didn't work. There were a few nibbles but I didn't land any fish.

> I didn't know how lonely I was
> until I met him.
> I said, "I am divorced."
> He said, "His loss is
> some other man's gain."
> I answered, too honestly,
> "there is no other man"
> and hoped there might be.
> He was silent then
> and forever, after.

ELLEN: Yes. Men are often afraid of getting involved. I know how you felt to be rejected.

MARY: Do you?

> Humiliating
> to wait
> at fifty
> for a call
> for a word
> for a kiss
> from a man
> hardly known,
> pushing aside
> proven women,
> fine friends,
> to chase
> his scent,
> knowing
> it is better
> to wait
> for a call
> never coming
> than not
> to wait
> or want
> at all.

LISA: Do you still feel that way?

MARY: No, at least not often. I accept my singleness. It happened rather suddenly.

> Once, passing a certain place
> I joyously contemplated
> being there
> then realized
> it was the sort of place
> my husband and I
> had often been
> together.
>
> For the very first time
> I really knew
> what all those legalities
> had failed
> to teach.
>
> My marriage was as dead
> as my youth
> and all my mourning
> and seeking
> would not bring
> them back

Since then I have gained strength. Joining this support group has helped. It was good I did because I had a set-back when my boss fired me to hire a young, pretty secretary.

> We will
> work hard
> for low wages
> gratefully BUT
> THEY much prefer
> our daughters and
> even granddaughters.
>
> The unwanted cringe
> our backs ache
> our eyes dull
> we even stop
> thinking we

are worth
HIRING.

JENNIFER: I remember. You were pretty depressed then. We had to help restore your self confidence. We nagged you to get some training for a better job.

MARY: It wasn't easy but I did take the courses. And you all encouraged me through them and through the awful job search. You, Jennifer, gave me a good lead that led to a new job. It's lucky I changed jobs because at my new place there are other women alone. Doing things with them helps me cope with the Noah's Ark Syndrome.

> They are still coming
> two by two off the ark.
>
> Hostesses do not invite
> unescorted single women
> divorcees or even widows
> expecting they will rape
> husbands, steal homes or,
> worst trauma of all, mean
> an odd number at table.
>
> What kind of orgies
> need such pairings?

ELIZABETH: You make me feel terrible. It's true I haven't often included my widowed women friends when my husband and I invite our coupled friends over. But I really thought the singles would be uncomfortable. It isn't that I didn't want them. As a matter of fact, sometimes when I do ask one, she refuses to come because she would be the only single. It's a two way street.

Well, I'm sorry I interrupted you but I had to say that.

I was wondering, did you finally get used to the city?

MARY: It WAS hard that first winter. I didn't think I would make it. But I did.

I rushed to the ocean
during the February thaw
to find dried sea grass
waving tall and golden
undefeated by the storms.
There by the shore
I danced with the grass
exulting at my strength
to bear aloneness,
shouting to the grass
"we have weathered
the winter
you and I
we are kin
we are kin
we are kin."

I felt proud of coping.

I have learned
to blow the horn
threaten landlords,
utility companies,
and meter maids,
use public parks,
thrift shops,
and free clinics,
insult insulters,
ignore accosters,
trust strangers,
when feasible
see rainbows
in the gutters
find in alleys
parking spaces
boxes for bookcases
wild flowers
even furniture.

Now I sleep through
neighbors' parties,
drown out trucks

with Beethoven,
fix doorknobs,
outwit pay toilets,
swim at hotels
though not registered.

A new city kid
at fifty
learns fast.

Well, I am sorry I took so long to tell my story. Virginia, here's the button.

(Mary passes the button to Virginia.)

VIRGINIA: I'm glad things are better now, Mary. I used to think being divorced was easier than being widowed. When someone dies you blame yourself. You say, "what did I do wrong?" You feel guilty for living.

MARY: Women blame themselves for divorce too. They ask, "what did I do wrong to make him behave that way?" They even blame themselves when their children get divorced. Since we have so little power in the world, we over exaggerate our importance in the family which is the only place many of us are allowed to feel important.

VIRGINIA: I guess so. Anyway, I know a lot of women lose husbands through divorce or death. There are lots of widows around because men marry younger women and die younger. But it seemed at first as if I was the only one. I understand, Mary, about your letter to a suburbanite. We were best friends with our neighbors and after Ralph's death it seemed:

Wherever I went
they were always together
She was the echo
of his steps
and he drew in her closeness
like a fragrance.
Silent and close,
they dreamt by the fire
spent as the embers.
simple with loving.

Watching their unison,
I yearned
for moments
that never again
would be
for me, for me, for me.

Oh, I did my share of crying too. I suppose it is good I did.

If I had to give advice to others I'd say:

When a loved one is dying
go into the woods and cry.
Only pure beauty
like the sight of sun on water
or birdsongs in loved trees
that he will never share again
will bring those tears
for his darkness and yours.

The clumsy comfort of friends
and the strange running
or bargaining you will do,
will only make a tighter vise
about your throbbing head
and angry throat.

Go alone to beauty.
Mourn your aloneness and weep
for the loved one
and for yourself
and for the fragility of life
when the world shared
is so beautiful.

In the end we are all alone
but there is still beauty;
it is eternal
and so are memories
alive in us.

For me the memory of Ralph is very strong. I am not a single at heart. I can't go to bars or clubs like some women alone do seeking to end singleness, at least for one night.

I know times have changed but I haven't.

> I suppose I am still his.
> Sometimes I have thought
> the pressure of another body
> would wipe away his imprint
> but my desire flows backward
> stubborn as the tide
> to the wedding bed
> so I wear his ring still,
> cursing the throat lump
> that certain music brings.

MARY: Weren't you ever angry at what happened to you?

VIRGINIA: Certainly.

> Once I baked bread
> and because I had
> to eat it alone,
> threw half
> into the yard
> for the dogs.

I even went through a period of isolation and self pity. I shut myself away, thinking:

> Plants are more predictable
> than people.
> If you give plants
> enough water
> light and warmth
> they will reward you.
>
> People, on the other hand,
> even given
> considerable attention,

> may forget you
> or become hostile
> or even die
> Begonias are better.

I was actually mad at my children and grandchildren for being occupied with their own lives. I hated the empty nest. I felt:

> I had no home
> there was no love in those walls
> which enclosed my grief
> no comfort in plants and colors
> with which I tried to deceive.

> There cannot be a home for one
> where there had been many.
> A woman alone becomes an orphan
> crying in the night
> with only cold walls to hear.

ELLEN: You seem alright now. It is hard to believe you were like that. How did you get to feeling better?

VIRGINIA: I'm not sure. Maybe time. Maybe my need and strength to survive.

> One day I was ready
> to give up
> what seemed
> an impossible life.

> The next day
> there was light
> and air
> and energy.
> The dark had gone
> as quickly as it came.

> I could exult
> again at music
> and at the sight
> of sun on snow.

The papers
I had thrown about
to signal my despair
could be put in neat
and manageable piles.

I could do
what needed
to be done
and what before
seemed a task
beyond endurance.

Even though I had lost him
I would not wear black
and put on Spring colors
being as I was meant to be.

Yesterday I mourned.
Today I have life to celebrate
I have myself.

I realized it was not my fault Ralph was dead and that he would want me
to enjoy life. I began to do things and take as many trips as I could afford.
If not now, when? I am luckier financially than many widows.

At the slightest invitation
I bed down in strange cities.
From my lair in Bedford Square
I took London in a week.
Paris is my harem now
and Aberdeen and Amsterdam
and Bath and Berkeley too.

New York and Washington are mine
I have dallied with Chicago,
San Francisco and Tucson,
Puerto de la Cruz and Marrakesh
I do not love you less
because I made Atlanta mine.

If I cannot have lovers
I shall have cities.
Sixty cannot be coy
as twenty with lovers
waiting in the wings.
I go boldly to conquer cities
Who is to judge of consummations
and compensations?

I also decided when home to get out daily for exercise and seeing people.
I joined the "Y" and began to use the pool.

We are sweatless
and weightless
purity personified,
our rhythmic motion
comforting as we
unite with fluids
of our individual
and species birth.

We are grateful
for oceans
lakes and pools
where body merges
intimately with
perfect medium
so even those
unlucky or clumsy
everywhere else
glide and hide
gracefully into
crystal refuge.

ELLEN: Swimming works off sexual energy too.

VIRGINIA: Yes, I know. If they knew how sensuous swimming was, they might ban
                it. I am in the exercise class at the "Y" too. Also, I made some terrific new
                women friends there including Elizabeth whom I brought tonight to
                this group. Elizabeth is a dedicated, almost full time volunteer at the "Y"
                and other places. She got me into volunteering and that helped me too.
                The least I could do was get her into this group. And, now the least I

could do is give Elizabeth her turn to talk.

(She hands Elizabeth the button.)

ELIZABETH: Well, I've been listening to all your troubles and feel lucky that at seventy I still have my husband. He is special--a truly faithful and kind man. Not all men are like your ex, Mary. Our marriage has lasted fifty years. So far we have our health, are enjoying life and can help others. It feels good to be seventy.

> Seventy is being outside
> on a November day
> knowing the fragility
> of sunshine.
>
> Seventy is facing lost causes
> and fighting on
> having little to lose.
>
> Seventy is loss
> and dry tears unseen
> but also passion
> and private jokes
> suddenly revealed by life.
>
> Seventy is waking early
> to seek treasures
> which there is no room
> to hold.
>
> Seventy is sensing
> which stranger
> will give the ecstasy
> of friendship
> and who will betray.
>
> At seventy
> you grasp wisdom
> in your hands
> while they
> are still strong.

> Go into seventy
> hoping and loving
> you will be women
> made beautiful
> by having lived
> well and long.

VIRGINIA: You give me courage to get older.

ELIZABETH: Thanks. I've decided what is important in life. We tend to obsess sometimes about nothings. I'm beyond that now.

> Having climbed the mountain,
> I came down the other side
> carrying carefully mementoes
> collected with great effort
> going up.
>
> Halfway down I stopped
> and suddenly hurled away
> those no longer treasures
> amazed I had cherished
> such burdens.

I have learned to live for each day and be grateful for it. We women are lucky because we love to nurture and can nurture through life, though not always in the same way we did once. I love being a senior volunteer and I love days like the one I had at the beach last May.

> I lust for the ocean.
> In May when sunners huddle,
> with shawls on the beach,
> I swim the waves alone
> warm with joy.
>
> My sole ownership was challenged
> when Amy, seven and a half,
> introduced herself
> and asked how to float.
>
> "Don't be afraid
> and you won't sink," I said.

She replied, "I'll play dead."
"Not dead," I told her,
"just relax--the water holds."

Neither of us cold
seventy swam with seven.
I taught her how to float
while her parents sunned
and Amy stroked my toes
in gratitude, teaching love.

Wherever you go, Amy
I shall go.
In the Spring you are seventy,
you will recall
how a May swimmer
taught you courage.

Though I shall be long gone
I will live then in you
my child and my sister.

Yes, life is good. The only thing I worry about is that my health may fail or that Jim will get sick, or that I will become senile.

Even my children grow old
I see my years
written on their once soft faces
now wise and worn.

I hope at eighty I can still do the things I love. Dora, what is it like to be eighty?

(She hands the button to Dora.)

DORA: You are the same as you have always been, a little achey sometimes and slower and forgetful. Yet within you are all the things you ever were and more.

Two years past eighty
I forget a lot of things
I don't want to remember

like watching my words.
I remember a lot of things
I thought I had forgotten
like Miss Brown
who made kindergarten
another home.

Two years past eighty
I own my old body
with all its imperfections
and like myself.

Two years past eighty
I spot a new bird
learn a wildflower's name
see a great grandchild smile
hear live, for the first time,
Bach's Sonata in C Major,
tell the President off,
drink a new wine,
and make new friends
of you.

There are lots of good things. However, the bad thing is some people
don't see YOU at all. They see only age and reject and belittle you
because of that. It makes me furious when they talk to me as if I were a
child. Mad turned inward becomes sad so I express my anger. I say to
the world:

I am in this old body
but not of it.
My mind runs barefoot
unwinded along the ocean
and my spirit climbs
mountains.

Who are you
to judge me unfit
and unlovable
when I so love
this world
and human touch?

You know some people never touch old people as if they are repulsive. When I was in the hospital, I noticed that the interns and medical students stood practically across the room from me. And they couldn't wait to get out of the room. It was different for young patients. Old folks have the same needs as other people for closeness. I let them know how I felt about it. I'll make a prediction:

> I will leave as I came
> screaming pain.
> I shall not accept with grace
> the indignities of age
> and the indignities to age
> but exit--not too soon--
> decrying my doom,
> hating my fate,
> protesting my loss,
> pushing back the end,
> with every angry breath.

ELIZABETH: I like what you said. I admire your guts. I need to learn how to be eighty in a world insensitive to older people. Can you be specific about how to handle folks when they treat us as stupid because we are old.

DORA: I'll give you an example.

> The electric company
> overcharges me
> but there is nowhere else
> I can buy electricity.
> I call to complain
> they yes me
> but still overcharge.
>
> I will keep calling
> and talking.
> How much an hour
> do they pay
> their telephone clerks?

ELIZABETH: Not bad. It gives me some ideas.

VIRGINIA: I know what Dora and Elizabeth mean about ageism. I feel it already at sixty and get angry too.

MARY: Certainly at fifty you experience it, as I told you.

ELLEN: And at forty.

JENNIFER: Even at thirty, the double standard of aging exists. Men and employers bypass you for the twenty year olds.

LISA: At college, many senior men preferred the freshman girls.

DORA: Ageism is a common disease. You learn to live with it but you should try hard to do what you can about it. Don't wait until my age to fight ageism. Also, more young women have to prepare for aging by getting to know older women. I'm glad I have you all as friends. I lost my husband and many friends to death. A few of my friends older than I do not recognize me. But I have come to some reconciliation with my losses.

> No love is lost
> even though the lover
> turns away from us
> or life.
>
> Within us are the people
> we have loved,
> not as they were
> but as we wanted
> them to be.
>
> As our fresh grief
> softens to sorrow,
> we suddenly discover
> the lover's eyes
> in our mirror
> the lover's words
> on our lips,
> even the beloved's jokes
> have become ours.
>
> What reality has taken,
> we have taken

for our own.
Nothing is ever lost.
Layers of our being
contain all that has
lived for us
or that we imagined.

We exude
the strength
of our losses
and our gains glow
even in the dark.

All in all, friends, being eighty or even ninety or one hundred is not bad considering the alternative.

I'm alive
I'm well
I survive
I survive well.

Well, to survive as well as I do, ladies, I need my rest. I think it is time to end this meeting. If anyone has anything else to say, you better do it fast.

(She gets up and gives the button to Lisa.)

Lisa stands and says:

I'm alive
I'm well
I survive
I survive well.

Jennifer stands and says:

I'm alive
I'm well
I survive
I survive well.

Ellen stands and says:

> I'm alive
> I'm well
> I survive
> I survive well.

Mary stands and says:

> I'm alive
> I'm well
> I survive
> I survive well.

Virginia stands and says:

> I'm alive
> I'm well
> I survive
> I survive well.

Elizabeth stands and says:

> I'm alive
> I'm well
> I survive
> I survive well.

The seven women say in unison:

> We will rest together on our ambivalences.
> We will share islands
> as we struggle
> toward an uncharted shore.

(The seven women carry their pillows off the stage.)

END OF ACT ONE

ACT TWO

Scene I

Women Who Can't Rest on Their Ambivalences

Note: this scene consists of four short vignettes with each set of characters entering and exiting from the stage. Should the theater have spotlights, and the stage be large enough, the stage may be pre-set for these episodes, with the actresses in place, and the lights turned on the appropriate spots when each vignette is enacted. There are no props for thin and fat self. There is a glass and bar stool for the second encounter, two chairs for the psychiatrist's scene and a bench for the jail cell. Suitable substitutions or additions may, of course, be made, such as a large mirror for thin and fat self.

VIGNETTE ONE: THIN SELF AND FAT SELF

(Two women enter, both the same age, same hairdo and color hair, but one thin, one fat.)

(Holding hands, facing audience, they recite in unison the following:)

> Not all of us can rest on our ambivalences. Our ambivalences
> make us rest-less.
>
> > Two lunches
> > one lean
> > one rich
> > one for thin me
> > one for fat me.
> >
> > Which is real me?

Which is good me?
Which is bad me?
Which shall I be?
this year
next year
always?

How boring
it must be
to be
in the same flesh
forever.

I can be
she or me
fleet seductress
or slow sweet
earth mother.
We have more clothes
or disguises
than anyone.
Thin me
in baby blue
and pink.
Fat me
in black and blue.

Two lunches
two wardrobes
two lives
two selves
two cages
too much
too bad
too sad.

The world
does not know
who I am
nor do I really
know which
is me.

We have been
every size.
We know how
everyone feels.
We are
everyone.

(Fat self pulls away her hand angrily and facing thin self says:)

This twin-ing bores me.

There you are
clothed in your thinness
elegance understated
by my over stated presence
socially berated
and self hated
with audience deceived
by my laughter.

Fat me
seems big and powerful.
Outside a threat
but weak from tears
unshed.

THIN SELF:

Thin me asserts
appears, allows
accepts applause.

Thin me, though outside
self-confident,
efficiency personified,
can be destroyed
by the slightest threat.
Then she hides
in the fat woman.

FAT SELF:

Fat me resents
returns, reminds

reclaims, re-enacts
retreats.

Fat me has
seized a large space
in this world
but has not
filled her emptiness.

For griefs and injuries,
she takes candy bars
ice cream, loaves of bread
chewing anger.

Where but inward
can her anger go?
Like an armadillo's armor
she layers pain
upon her body
making her body
a fortress.

Nothing shall reach
her there
or tempt her out.

THIN SELF: The tense cheekbones know
the aching jaw knows
the thumping heart knows
the tight breath knows
the rising fluids know
what mind and mouth deny.

That fat woman
is going to kill me
unless I kill her first.
Which will it be
she or me?

Can I reason with her?
Can she remember?
Coming out of fat

I find a forgotten self
in my closet
light, lithe dresses.

Coming out of fat
I salute the mirror
and old friend.
The moat collapses
around a weighty enemy
suddenly a stranger.

Coming out of fat
I run the stairs
with breath to spare
and dream of dashing
through open fields
to celebrate Spring.

FAT SELF: That's easy when you're not depressed.

Do you know what depression is?

It crawls out of bed with you
grayer than the darkest morning.
Even three cups of hot coffee
and the warm, scented bath
cannot shake the chill.

Wherever you may go or run,
it goes along, unwelcomed.
Reject it, but it shares your day,
your friends, your food and work,
its voice louder in stillness
but heard above all distraction.

There are those blessed times
when finally untwined and free
you celebrate your gratitude
incredulous the parasite persisted
determined never to host it again
and all the angrier when
the twin returns to share again

your bed, your day, your strength.

THIN SELF: You sound desperate.

FAT SELF: I am.

> Having more hope
> or responsibility
> or lacking the courage
> of Sylvia or Anne,
> I kill myself
> in increments,
> inches of obesity
> strangling heart,
> self-esteem
> and womanhood.
>
> Running always,
> yet almost unable to move,
> I move to food
> seeking and denying life
> in one gesture
> of anger and supplication.
>
> The consumed consumes.
> Too much demanded
> too little returned.
> I will take mine
> even unto sickness
> monstrosity and death.

THIN SELF: You have one litany you repeat like a frog's croak. In fact, I think you have a frog fetish:

> You bought frogs,
> indoor frogs,
> outdoor frogs
> frogs for your bath
> and the birdbath
> a kitchen frog
> and a frog
> signalling

in your window.
Even your daughter
bought you a frog
at rest.

Was it that
bloated beyond
recognition,
you are sister
to the frogs
or rather
that you desire
a frog prince
to rescue you
although
you know
fairytales
are for the young
and foolish?

(The two rejoin hands and recite in unison.)

Sometimes I wish
I could destroy
one me
or both
in one long binge
or lake water.

Well me
sick me
live me
dead me
which she
will it be?

Two lunches
one for thin me
one for fat me
which is real me
which is good me
which is really me

> which shall I be
> this year
> next year
> always?

(Arms linked, Thin and Fat Self leave the stage.)

VIGNETTE TWO: IN A BAR

(Helene enters carrying a bar stool and sits on it. She holds a glass. Mary enters, and looks at her for a minute.)

MARY: It is ironic, Helene was voted most likely to succeed by our class but when she came to the 25th reunion she was a mess. She was one of the first of us to marry but her successful, brilliant husband turned out to be a mean bastard and alternated between abusing and ignoring her and the kids. She is still with him but their marriage is rotten. As for Helene:

> Voice husky
> from gin and tobacco
> my girlhood friend
> sits across the room
> telling of troubles
> unbearable and
> borne in bars.
>
> Wherever we go,
> she must pause
> for a drink.
> Her smoke combines
> with my tears
> so that I can
> barely see her
> and wonder,
> not without anger,
> if she I loved
> is still inside.
>
> I try hard
> not to hate

this now stranger
destroyed by life
and by her remedies.

HELENE: *(lights a cigarette)*

We walking wounded
triaged to ourselves
barely visible
living alone
or with cats
or catastrophic people
are humans too.

Oh, I have sought
belongingness
but nowhere
have I found a home
except these bars
where I buy a seat.
Those who do not belong
long for companionship.
Even Thoreau left Walden.

Full circle
I come
from loneliness and pain
to this circle my glass
and doubled pain.

Life which withheld
may yet give
and so can be trusted.
Life which destroyed
is a buzzard.
One runs from buzzards
or your flesh is theirs.

(Helene holds up glass)

Peter, who is to say
I do not love you well

because another lover
wooed and won?

MARY:

Too many yesterdays
creep into todays.
Her clock is clogged
with soggy memories
unresolved and
unresolvable.

Her clock threatens
to stop
and she to stop it.

She who raced
against time
is running
out of time.

(Mary leaves the stage.)

(Helene drains her glass and slowly weaves off the stage.)

Vignette Three: Psychiatrist's Office

(A woman in a white physician's coat enters followed by Catherine, about 50. The psychiatrist puts two chairs on the stage and sits on one and motions to Catherine to sit on the other. Catherine huddles in the chair slumped over, very still and withdrawn. The psychiatrist reads from her notebook as if reading a case report to herself.)

PSYCHIATRIST:

Battered enough
she braced
for another blow
and when
it did not come
remained frozen
waiting.

Let me review the case history. She was referred to me by her internist because she kept getting physical symptoms with no organic cause. She was brought up like many women of her generation to be good and to be a lady under all circumstances.

> She drank the draft diluted.
> Emotions too were muted
> in patterns primly suited
> to lull each living note.
>
> She walked in paths soft lighted
> and passion's fire was slighted
> for fear her heart once sighted
> would rising sear her throat.
>
> She said she was contented.
> Beneath, her pain fermented
> as heart and soul resented
> her holding life remote.

PSYCHIATRIST: *(turns to Catherine)*
How are you feeling, Catherine?

CATHERINE:
> Like walking alone
> in November
> on rotted oak leaves
> in cold rain
> at midnight
> knowing winter
> will close
> you in soon
> and forever.

PSYCHIATRIST: That bad!

CATHERINE:
> They will find me there
> in my unclean house
> by the stink of my rot
> wafted through closed doors
> and bolted windows.

PSYCHIATRIST: I am sorry you feel so terrible.

NASHUA PUBLIC LIBRARY

CATHERINE:

My parents told me
not to cry.
You said I could.
I cry now
for pains frozen
a half century.

I walk across
the bridge to Tuesdays
where I have a life
within a life
that turns to reality
to drama mused upon
with you who I beg
to love me a little
or pretend you do.
Let me love you
in a life within
a life of shadow.

PSYCHIATRIST:

I know I have become important to you in our time together. I do care.
But you need to make a life in the real world.

CATHERINE:

Nests are hard to come by
and fledgling fliers
often fall
to unreceptive ground.

Full grown, I staggered frozen to your doorstep where warm, protected
from the storm outside, I dared the storm within--seeing in your eyes
unfaltering stars and in your hands barriers against that fatal, final
misstep into the charm always underfoot and calling.

To leave the doorstep of an imperfect mother with only young fears is
hard enough. To leave the doorstep of a perfect mother with adult
knowledge of the raging storms is too much to ask.

I do not trust life or myself, only you.
I cry "stay with me always; I am afraid."
But you offer me a paradox.
To earn your approval and my own
I must give you up.

I have to learn to conjugate
to verb to be
in the first person singular
and the present tense.

PSYCHIATRIST: That's right. You have to work on your life in the world outside this office. You have a lot to offer in the real world.

CATHERINE:
I shall be free as you would have me free
and armed enough to bear the pain of parting
and leaving you, to go on with hope to see
this present tense of life now starting.

Though now I stand against the door
reliving history once more
please know I will not drag your light
into the grave where I have lived so long.

Please wait until I feel by day and night
that I am for once and I am strong.

PSYCHIATRIST: I understand what you are asking me so movingly. But unfortunately we do have to deal with reality, even here. You have more strength than you know. I am sorry but your health insurance is used up for psychiatric treatment. I know you cannot afford the fees I have to charge because of my realities. The next session will have to be our last. We will talk then about how you will manage. I will give you a list of self help groups in the area and also of social agencies which have low fees. We will say a proper goodbye. Now our hour is up, regretfully. I hate to push you out but another patient is waiting.

CATHERINE: Thank you.

PSYCHIATRIST: *(gets up and walks to edge of stage.)*
That was painful. I'm exhausted. I hated doing that. But I can't work for nothing. I must support myself. I tried hard. She's better than when she came. At least I haven't made her drug-dependent. She feels better physically. Before, she was headed for unnecessary surgery. She could have used more therapy. But there are so many others waiting, so many casualties. They keep slipping on the ice, and there seems to be nobody out there sanding the streets.

I have needs too. Patients expect more of women doctors and I suppose of other women professionals. And they get angrier at women than at men when we can't deliver everything forever. The Catherines see us as perpetual nurturers but we are only human.

> Each woman's
> pregnant face
> invites
> seduction
> rejection
> always.

> My breast is empty
> My ear is tired.
> Please take
> endless troubles
> other places.
> Help yourself.
> Be quiet.
> Manage.

> For now
> I am out of
> chicken soup
> and the only client
> for my couch
> is me.

(Psychiatrist leaves the stage quickly.)

(Catherine leaves the stage slowly.)

VIGNETTE FOUR: IN JAIL

(Enter Sara, Consuelo, Lois, Beth and Sister Mary Caritas. They wear peace buttons. They sit on a bench.)

SARA: They want us to post bail and get out of here but we won't. They put us in jail for protesting the missiles and we'll stay here to make people aware.

CONSUELO: Yes we must do what we can to stop a war. We'll stay.

LOIS: Agreed. But the dirt in this cell is awful and I need a bath.

BETH: Agreed. But it is very annoying to have those guards keep yelling dyke. It is also maddening that the newspapers keep diverting attention from our anti-war protest to snicker that I am a lesbian. They don't bother mentioning that you, Sara, are married and you, Lois, have a male lover and Consuelo is a widow.

SARA: Beth, you forget they keep writing about my kids being at home unmothered while I am here in jail. They forget the kids have a father. The truth is they don't see women at all as full people. They trivialize the causes we believe in and don't take our political actions seriously. They simply point to our sexuality, whether heterosexual or homosexual, and to our mother role as if that is our only identity.

BETH: You're right.

LOIS: To tell the truth, when they don't take us seriously, even I, sometimes, in weak moments, begin to wonder why we put ourselves on the line for a cause that is probably lost anyway. They keep building the nukes and the weapons and starting wars no matter what we do.

SARA: I think we'd better remind ourselves why we are here.

CONSUELO: That would be good.

SISTER CARITAS: It would help me also to seek why we are here. The bishop's lawyer wanted to pay a fine and release me. I want to come to the truth of it. Was I wrong to do what I did and to stay here?

BETH: Okay, let's talk about it. You first Sara.

SARA: It may sound dramatic when I tell you how I feel but I feel that way.

> A life needs goals to stretch toward.
> I saw in my children's soft young faces
> my mission and my goal.
> I would give them love
> and the world would be theirs.

I kissed each warm and precious cheek
but when I recognized
what the world really is,
I pulled away in shock
to find the death heads cold beneath.

I saw my Jewish children's children
marching to the gas ovens
all bringing with them little goals
like worn out toys to bed.

I also saw that
as we stockpile neutron bombs
which destroy only life, not property,
children stroll slowly home from school
through radioactive rain
carrying mutated, defective genes
clutching schoolbooks celebrating war
yearning for uniforms and guns
holding already congealed concepts
of we and they--properly socialized
made too stupid to love.

During Vietnam
our children
burnt villages, burnt flesh.

The generals tell us
international relations
are too complex for us.
It is hard even to remember the names
that separate us into nationhood.
But I know we shall have peace
only if we wish it enough.

Mothers have a special responsibility to work for peace. That is why I am here.

LOIS: It's interesting that you, a Jew, and I, a Christian, are close in values. Some of the things you just said could have been written by a person who inspired me, Dr. Albert Schweitzer. He was a Christian clergyman, physician and winner of the Nobel peace prize twenty-five years ago.

He said "the spirit is a mighty force for transforming things". He also said "we shall have peace only when we want peace" and have "reverance for life" and "rediscover the fact that we all together are human beings."

Some of us awakened even before Vietnam. My revulsion for war started during World War II.

> As a young Red Cross volunteer
> I walked daily through trains
> of three-tiered stretchers
> with mutilated men, my age then,
> glad to leave the killings
> but never young again.
> I also walked through trains
> of caskets.
> I walk there still.
>
> Later, after Vietnam,
> my student veterans
> wept to me their despair and guilt.
> It was our guilt too.

In this time of fatal irreverance for life, this Christian joins with you, Sara, a Jew. We both belong to what Schweitzer called "the fellowship of those who bear the mark of pain." He meant by that those who have felt hurt, can empathize with hurt, help to heal hurt and end the hurting. That is why I am here.

BETH:

> I suppose I am anti-war
> because I am a physician
> I have glimpsed the wonders
> of the cell and human body
> so marvelous and beautiful
> that even brilliant scientists
> aren't sure how it all works.
> But a bullet can stop life instantly.
> Lungs are a marvel of design
> but fallout destroys a million lungs.
>
> Between the wars
> they mourn the dead

and hide the wounded
and speak of peace
meanwhile arming.

You know one semester while in medical school, during the winter break I went to St. Augustine, Florida. There is an old fort there, the Fort of San Marco, which is beautiful. It's right on the bay. Ferns grow in the furnaces which were used in colonial times to heat cannonballs to set enemy ships afire. Now, people sit peacefully on the walls enjoying the beauty of the old walls, the birds and water. It is a tamed fort. My dream is that all the energy that goes into war preparation and war itself can be channelled into preserving and enhancing life. As a physician, my job is to conserve life and nuclear war may destroy it utterly. That is why I am here. Sister, why are you here?

SISTER CARITAS: Well, you all know that the work our Lord gave me to do was to run a city kitchen that feeds those no one else will feed. Lately, with the high un-employment we have had so many more people coming--including fine proud people. They are ashamed because they can't get work though it is not their fault. People of all religions and kinds ask us for all types of help besides food because many government and government subsi-dized social services have been cut or eliminated. The government is spending our money on arming itself and other countries. I needed to come to the truth of why such a rich country can not take care of its own people and why countries all over the world are impoverishing their people also to stockpile armaments when indeed there are enough mu-nitions now to destroy civilization.

I prayed and prayed to understand and for help for the world. Then one day during Mass I felt God wanted women to say the time had come to end war and preparation for war. So I joined you on the picket line. And when they told us to leave, I stayed with you. And when they dragged you to the police van, I refused to move also. So they took me to the van too. I noticed that they carried me gently though, and I prayed for you who were being handled roughly. I pray also for those Nuns, Sisters of mine in Christ, who have been killed and suffered abominations for their war and for the people.

CONSUELO: Thank you for your prayers, Sister. I guess it is my time to tell why I am here. I will not say it as well as you who have more education. I had to go to work very early and worked all my life in factories, even when my children were small. There was not time for books. My husband did hard labor. He died young, worn out. My children are grown now and I have only myself to take care of but I feel I must have care for the world.

There has not been much work in my city lately. The shoe factory where I worked for twenty years closed. The only job I could get was making parts for the bombers that America supplies other countries to use in their wars and that our government buys to prepare for war. I didn't like doing this work but I had to eat and pay my rent and help my neighbors.

I've always been a hard worker and last month they decided to give me twenty cents extra an hour because I was so fast. Can you imagine twenty cents when the company makes so much money on those government contracts? Anyway, one night I saw on television the dead and terribly wounded people after a bombing raid. Some looked like my children. I couldn't eat, I couldn't sleep. They next day I told my boss to keep the twenty cents extra an hour and the job. I would not anymore make weapons to kill people. I took a bus to your city hoping to find work that was not bloody. I happened to pick up one of your anti-war leaflets on the street. It had Sara's phone. I called Sara. I joined you in picketing. I must do what I must do to face myself. I love this country but not what it is doing now.

LOIS: It was good to share. I feel better, reinforced.

(Sara, Lois, Consuelo, Beth and Sister Caritas stand and recite together.)

> We are in the middle of
> war and peace,
> radicalism and conservatism
> private concern and political action
> activism and retreatism
> convenience and the environment
> our country and universality.
>
> We WILL MAKE SPLASHES
> as we thrust
> with other women
> toward a shore uncharted
> but not denied
> by us.

(End of Vignette Four and end of Scene One, Act Two.)

Scene II:

Questioning and Celebrating

(The entire cast comes onto the stage and the small groups who have been in scenes together sit in separate clusters on the floor. As each person speaks, she stands and when through speaking, sits again.)

MARY:

Strong trees break
when the storm hits hard,
Why do I go on
waving those branches
like a fool or a beckoner?

LISA:

Those of us going into marriages
and those of us coming out of marriages
pause as we pass, asking
why such strains?

Those of us going into jobs
and those of us coming out of jobs
look each other in the eyes
with deep compassion.

JENNIFER:

Who shall protect us
from these spiders
these managers
these leaders
who spin papers and words
in such corrupt webs?

Where shall we go

70

to dream those dreams
to keep us from the sewers
and the grave?

LOIS:
Why do most jobs
why do many marriages
alienate men and women
from each other
and themselves?

ELLEN:
I don't know. I only know that:

I came into this isolation
knowing that before we parted
we lay body to body
man and woman together
unclothed and unmasked
in our need for comfort
yet could take none from each other
for more than a moment--
a moment I recall weeping
for what might have
strengthened us
instead of sending us
to weep alone.

Why, when life is loss
and humans fragile,
don't we cling together
instead of blaming those
we love the most?

How can we revenge ourselves
upon the world
instead of upon each other
or ourselves?

LISA:
It's so sad.

Somewhere
someone
somehow

something
soon
please.

SARA: The somewhere is here.

The someone is ourselves, sisters.
The somehow is direct action
The something is unity.
The soon is now.

There is no time for waiting
No strength to spend on tears.
There is no place for forgetting
or seeking escape from the world.
We can't shield ourselves.
We must wield power.

ELIZABETH: I admire you, Sara, but women don't have much power now. Not all of us are able or ready to go to jail for our convictions. Some of us take care of the everyday. I take care of my ninety-four year old mother who is frail in body and mind. Nobody else will do it. Women help as they can. Look at Dora:

She knows
where to find
hope, strategies
diversions
and even laughter.
Dora connects us
to herself
and each other.

DORA: Yes, I believe we are all connected, men and women and nature. In my life, I have seen how people have lost sight of that.

RUTH: Nature is important to me. Though my grandmother and mother lived in slums, they taught me to love the earth. In the crowded, dirty city, we always had plants blooming in the windows and on the fire escape. Strangers would wonder how mother and grandmother made so much light in tiny dark spaces. They didn't know they did it through love and a need to foster growth.

Marmita even stole for her plants. Our neighborhood had only cement and gravel. Marmita would have thought it funny that people now buy dirt in stores, what we call potting soil. She went to the park with a bag she sewed from a worn out coat and dug up loam from behind the rose bushes. "They won't miss it," she said.

Jane's dream was that someday she would have a farm in the country. Well, she never got her farm. But on summer nights she took me up to the roof of our apartment house and showed me the skies.

I haved always loved the moon. I remember, as an adolescent during World War II, being shocked to hear on the radio that there had been a successful bombing raid in those pre-radar days because the moonlight allowed pinpointing the targets.

Up until then, for me and many people, the moon had been a symbol of tranquility, peace, love, and womanhood. Well, then men landed on the moon and now the moon is a symbol of the space age which makes possible terrible weapons.

I think women should reclaim the moon. If you wouldn't think it silly, we could all come together in a circle and I could recite my womanchant about the full moon.

(The women, some more quickly than others, but all eventually link hands in a circle.)

RUTH:

Moon lit
moon struck
we gather
to celebrate
the full moon
in this full circle
our own
full moon.

We are moons
round
cyclic
constant
givers of light
sewers of buttons

fillers of cups.
We women
know circles.

We come
in ones and twos
and groups
for respite
share beauty
dreams, laughter
hopes
sorrows
tensions
fears
and in the sharing
gain courage
for another month.
For another struggle.

Full moon
full hearts
full house
full cups
full friends
full wombs
for some
full friends
full joy.

RUTH: Speak who you are.

(Each actress gives her real name and then says daughter of and gives her mother's name and then says granddaughter of and gives her grandmothers' names.)

RUTH: Moon lit
             moon struck
             we gather
             to celebrate
             the full moon
             in this full circle,
             our own

full moon
of women.

The world is a circle
it is our circle
our only circle
everyone's circle.

Speak of this
to those daughters and sons
who will follow.

DORA: Let's come closer together.

(The women come into a tight cluster. As they do, they raise their voices in laughter, in joy, in sorrow, in anger, in hope, in pain, in various words and tones, until the sound is overwhelming. They embrace.)

THE END

AUTHOR'S NOTE:

If discussion is desired, the leader might start the discussion by saying: "You are part of this poetic drama of women's voices. Are you in the middle? Are you in between? Who controls the tides? Do you rest on your ambivalences? Will you make splashes? Now it is your turn to talk about any feelings, thoughts, disagreements or anything else the play aroused in you."

The discussion leader should give the audience time and freedom to react rather than asking very specific questions as the reaction will vary according to the composition and needs of the audience.

The author would be grateful for any reports of audience comments or reactions or for suggested changes or additions in the play. See her address at the beginning regarding Performances and Royalties.